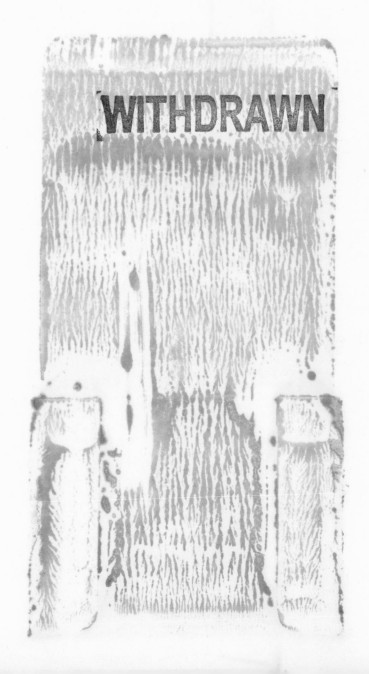

Raphael Soyer
fifty years of printmaking
1917–1967

Raphael Soyer

fifty years of printmaking

1917-1967

EDITED BY SYLVAN COLE, JR.

WITH A FOREWORD BY JACOB KAINEN

DA CAPO PRESS   NEW YORK, 1967

Da Capo Press
A Division of Plenum Publishing Corporation
227 West 17th Street, New York, N. Y. 10011

Library of Congress Catalog Card No. 67-29917
Printed in the United States of America

Foreword

Few of the leading American painters in this century have also maintained a lifelong interest in printmaking. During the past two decades more established painters than ever before have turned to making prints, but it is still too soon to estimate their staying power. Not many have shown the consistency and dedication of earlier painter-printmakers such as Childe Hassam, John Sloan, Arthur B. Davies, George Bellows, and Reginald Marsh. Of the painters who began making prints in the 1920's and 1930's, Raphael Soyer is one of the handful to maintain a consistent production throughout the intervening decades. This fully illustrated catalogue makes it clear that Soyer, in both the number and the quality of his prints, continues in the tradition of his distinguished American predecessors and belongs in their company.

As a painter Soyer's work is deceptively simple and straightforward. He paints the life around him, the life he has known. His subjects are himself, his friends, working men and women, derelicts, dancers, fellow painters, and models in his studio. All are painted in their immediate surroundings — in shops, streets, subways, buses, parks, studios. Their attitudes and gestures are natural — the women fasten skirts, pull up stockings, apply makeup, or simply relax; the men lounge on park benches or work at their trades. In this manner, Soyer gives a convincing image of everyday life. Consequently, he has often been considered a realist, but I think this description inadequate. True, he works from observed facts and to that extent his art is realistic; but drastic simplifications, an impulsive touch, and felicities of color give to his work a poetical and painterly quality that are superfluous to a realist. He is attracted to the physical reality of his subjects because the real world, naively speaking, forms the solid basis for transformations and inventions that can take place in the process of painting. His attitude toward life is deeply ingrained both as a man and a painter — if he prefers to paint a working girl rather than a society lady, it is not only because he feels a deeper sympathy for her, it is also because he finds her more interesting to paint.

Like other Russian-born American painters, including Arshile Gorky and John D. Graham, Soyer has studied the work of the masters with reverence and humility. He has generously acknowledged his debt to many artists, including Rembrandt, Goya, Corot, Degas, Eakins, Soutine, Kokoschka, Sloan, and Pascin, and, among his more immediate contemporaries, to Hopper and Levine. In his desire to live up to the standards of great painting, he has performed the historic role of striking deeper roots for representational painting in this country. This is an important contribution to our insular tradition. But the influences apparent in his own art are primarily general, more a matter of attitude than of style. Clearly, other artists have served only to strengthen his already developed purpose or to provide clues that would lead to greater freedom. Thus he has learned from Degas to give a casual appearance to his compositions and to strengthen the contour of a figure with a free line. From Rembrandt he has learned to simplify and subdue the hands, and Corot has confirmed his pleasure in the tender pulp of pigment. Pascin has given him the courage to treat the female model in a natural and sensuous way. But nowhere in Soyer's work is there any passage or compositional device that would point to a concrete influence. Soyer had his own main purpose from the start, which was to achieve tonal exactitude through the magical tempering of color, and to create the illusion of forms in light through the tautness and slackness of edges and surfaces. In this regard he shows a distant kinship with an artist not yet mentioned — Velasquez. The remarkable fact about Soyer is that, while he has yearned for the great qualities in painting, he has stubbornly retained his identity as an American and a New Yorker.

Breadth of drawing lies at the heart of Soyer's prints, as of his paintings. His drawing is direct, expressive, and without rhetoric. It suggests rather than describes, it gives the sense of structure without being anatomically explicit. His lines are loose, caressing, and spontaneous. The prints show the same motivations as the paintings, except that color and density of pigment are replaced by light, which spreads over his forms in a gentle shimmer that modifies tones and textures. It fills the rooms occupied by his subjects, creating intimate shadows and half-shadows. The mood is soft and tender, but the tones often are applied in vigorous flurries of lines. One of the surprises of his prints, in fact, is the delayed realization that the execution is so firm and incisive.

Soyer began making prints about 1917. He bought a small table-model etching press for twenty-five dollars and set it up in his family's tenement apartment. Soon he and fellow students at the National Academy were making rough prints. His subjects were members of his immediate family, himself, neighbors, and the city around him. These early efforts show qualities still apparent in his work — an honest and penetrating eye and full identification with his subjects. About 1920 he began to work in lithography, a medium for which he immediately showed an affinity. The early lithographs demonstrate a remarkable freedom of handling, rare in a youth of twenty. It was probably fortunate that up to 1930 his lithographs were executed on transfer paper, which does not permit careful rendering of tones. The subjects could thus be drawn broadly on the paper and then transferred to stones for printing. Some exceptionally fine prints resulted, among them the *Self-Portrait* (8), *Saul Berman* (9), and *Girl in Striped Sweater* (10).

In 1928–29, Soyer did a series of five street scenes (11–13, 15, 16) that are unique among his prints. They are drenched with the feeling of their locale, but are executed with a seemingly innocent eye. The figures are mere notations, the vehicles are slightly askew, and the houses, bridges, and other structures are negligently tilted. The simple and fanciful vision evident in these lithographs does not reveal the influence of other artists and probably stems from Soyer's Russian origins. The rearing horses in *East Side Street* (13), for example, which are treated in engaging silhouette, have the stiffly expressive character of folk art. At the time, in the late 1920's, Soyer was trying to fight off the influences of modern French masters, such as Cézanne and Van Gogh, who were being absorbed by his rebellious young associates. In the effort to remain himself, he relates,

... I really began from the beginning again and painted in a frank and almost naive manner subjects of ordinary interest that were part of my immediate life. ... At that time, I remember there was a flurry of discussion among the art critics as to whether or not this humor was conscious on my part. That was also the time, in the middle and late twenties, when Rousseau primitivism in art began to flourish here. Encouraged by a number of friends, I could have naturally embraced this naive style as my own and remained a permanent "primitive." But my eagerness to learn my craft and to widen the content of my paintings prevented me from acquiring the confining mannerisms of "primitive" art.[1]

This statement is significant not only because it indicates that Soyer has a natural tendency to simplify, but also because it describes the only real crisis in his art. He

[1] *Raphael Soyer,* (New York, American Artists Group, 1946), pp. 1–2.

resisted the easy temptation to achieve early success and chose the harder path, a decision that is characteristic of the man.

In 1933 he began to work directly on the stone, and a new quality became noticeable in his lithographs. He still drew with great freedom, but the fine hard surface made it possible to obtain an infinite variety of grays, to build up more richly textured darks, and to introduce needle and razor scratchings that allowed light to penetrate the tones. Thus a new quality, light, became the principal unifying element in his lithographs. With a deeper range of grays, the light areas became more pronounced, the edges of his forms more subtle, and the darks more differentiated. The new luminosity was immediately apparent in his first work on stone, *The Team* (23), in which the pattern of light, delicately modulated, carries out the rhythm of the design. The violinist and the dancer represent a contrast in rest and arrested motion, a motif that Soyer later used in different fashion in another of his finest prints, *Backstage* (36). Light again plays an important part in the following print, *The Model* (24), where the subject is illuminated complexly, with strong emphasis on the dissolving pattern of the dress along the curve of the lower back.

Soyer was fortunate at that time to have the services of a good artist-printer, Jack Friedland, who printed his stones throughout most of the twenties and the early thirties. Thus in his first two decades of work he did not have the handicap of contending with conservative printers who insisted that lithographs had to be drawn in a certain way to allow for proper printing. Many young artists of the period were cowed into careful rendering with the sharpened points of crayons, beginning with the hardest and finishing with the softest. Friedland finally had to give up his shop through lack of patronage, and Soyer's lithographic work was handled thereafter by the master printer, George C. Miller, and, more recently, by Miller's son Burr and by Irwin Hollander.

With the depression Soyer turned to subjects that reflected the poverty and unemployment around him. Actually, he did few prints that went much beyond the feeling for humanity he had shown from the beginning. He was an acute observer, and the implications of what he saw were undeniable; but he displayed none of the emotionalism of the more socially conscious artists. Most of his works in this special vein are in the nature of character studies, and one piece, *Waterfront* (34), is a lonely vista along which derelicts huddle. The fame of *The Mission* (27), which shows a group of homeless men with coffee and sandwiches, has given the mistaken impression that social themes were almost his exclusive concern in the thirties. Because it is a memorable image, widely reproduced, *The Mission* has come to represent the best in socially conscious printmaking of the period. There are other unsparingly observed subjects, such as *Bowery Nocturne* (28) and *Springtime* (56), which presents a number of people on park benches, but a substantial body of his work in the thirties centered around models in his studio.

The female model occupies a large place in Soyer's production. This is not solely because he is attracted to the charms of his subjects. The young woman in various states of dress or undress is a constant reminder that he is an artist. She is alien to the puritanical American tradition and holds him fast to his international heritage. She links him with Rembrandt, Corot, and Degas, and with Modigliani and Pascin in Montmartre. How many other American artists have done so many versions of female models, or done them so convincingly? What is American in Soyer's treatment is the fact that they are never idealized or generalized. He treats them as individuals while never losing sight of their desirability as women.

Some of his best female studies date from the early thirties. Among a number of vigorous lithographs, *Sylvia* (30) is particularly noteworthy for its breadth of handling. From the scribbles and scratches emerges a half-length nude, arms folded, with light burnishing her face and body. Nothing could be less glib. The success of the final image conceals the tireless working and reworking to achieve clarity of form and mobility of light. A year or so later he produced the magnificent *Backstage* (36), mentioned earlier. A young dancer in the center, flanked by two others, is in the act of turning to the viewer. The entire surface is thoroughly worked, with the darks and lights flawlessly placed.

Soyer joined the graphic section of the W.P.A. Federal Art Project in 1937 and remained for about a year. Among the prints produced during this period is a drypoint version of his early lithograph, *The Team* (23), reversed and with two figures added to make a new subject, *Backstage* (43). For the W.P.A. he produced eleven etchings and lithographs in all (43–53), mostly studies of old men, the most effective of which is the deeply felt *A Transient* (49). These prints renewed his interest in etching, and he created several fine plates in the late 1930's and early 1940's, including *Furnished Room* (48), which still echoes the depression.

The cohesiveness of Soyer's work as a whole hides the many changes and shifts in attack that have taken place over the years. No sharp breaks or "periods" are evident because in emphasizing new elements, the artist never abandoned his fundamental concerns. Yet it is clear that his most realistic period was from about 1935 to the early 1940's, and that the remainder of the forties was a time in which he gathered strength to reduce his naturalistic content, as he began to look with a fresh eye at the German Expressionists and at such other large-hearted artists as Munch, Kokoschka, and Soutine. As usual, no obvious trace of their influence is present, but Soyer's work, particularly in the prints, began to deepen and broaden.

In the 1950's, Soyer's production of prints took a sharp upswing, with 1954 the decisive year. A tendency to simplify planes, already noticeable in the *Casting Office* (65) of 1945, became more pronounced. This is evident in *The Window* (70) and *Boy and Girl* (72), and, most clearly, in *Dancers* (74), which has a classic feeling in its formal arrangement of curves and straight lines and its ample treatment of forms. At the same time a new depth of emotion becomes apparent — the emphasis is now on feeling rather than on the rendering of actualities. Among these semi-expressionist lithographs are *The Dancer* (77) of 1955, the intensely felt *Self-Portrait with Model* (81) of 1959–1960, and a number of studies of young models. Soyer's style and outlook remain the same, but a new restlessness becomes visible, a new desire to come closer to the core of his feeling.

In 1963 Soyer created a suite of sixteen etchings (89–104) which were published in 1965 by Associated American Artists in New York. The impressions were made by the master printer Emiliano Sorini. Some of the subjects are based upon Soyer's paintings but gain a separate identity from his fresh approach to the compositions. The *Self-Portrait* (89), which begins the set, is a miniature executed with great breadth and feeling. In this print we see, heightened, the consciousness of human mortality that is perhaps the true subject of Soyer's work as a whole. We see, also, the effort to conceal his skill, to feel his subject rather than to render it, to shun conspicuous deftness even at the risk of appearing crude. In other prints aquatint is introduced to make the light forms more telling, as in *Mother and Child* (89, II), *Pensive Girl* (101, II), and the classical *Young Woman* (95).

Soyer made occasional etchings in the next few years, including the *Self-Portrait with Wife* (107) of 1964. For economy of means and power of expression it is one of his finest prints. All of Soyer's virtues are here, reduced to their essentials. His self-portraits, honest and without illusion, have always been among his best works, but this etching has an uncalculated, trance-like quality and an impeccable justness of design.

During the past year Soyer has begun to vary his approach in lithography, working sometimes in line, with little tone added, and sometimes in lithotint washes. Lithotint is difficult to control because the grease content of the wash is unpredictable, but Soyer finds the unpredictability stimulating. He has made several highly personal works in the medium, including *Man and Wife* (119) and *Girl in Black Tights* (123), in both of which dark accents freely drawn with the brush make telling notes against the light washes.

This brief digest of Soyer's career as a printmaker barely indicates the range and quality of his work. Certainly it has an intensity and an unobtrusive originality that few American graphic artists in this century have equalled. Soyer has created a world of his own, one that parallels the life a generation has known. His art proves that modesty is a great virtue indeed, and that in the long run it usually holds its own with more heroic qualities. Corot said, "Delacroix is an eagle; I am only a skylark." But who can deny that the skylark now shares the same high place with the eagle?

Jacob Kainen
Consultant on Prints & Drawings
National Collection of Fine Arts
Washington, D.C.

Introduction

Surveying the fifty years of Raphael Soyer's printmaking has been a wonderful experience. Most books dealing with an artist's prints are compiled long after his death by hard-laboring researchers who attempt, as best as possible, to reconstruct what the artist actually did. Fortunately, we have been able to spend many hours with Raphael Soyer, to discuss with him all of his graphic output, to feel the warmth of his reaction at again seeing forgotten etchings and lithographs from his early years. These hours have been both enjoyable and enlightening, and we are grateful to Raphael Soyer, and to his wife, Rebecca, for being willing to devote so much time to documenting and confirming the information to be found in this catalogue.

Through the years, Raphael Soyer has kept a fairly complete file of his own work, and it is his personal collection that has served as the nucleus for this catalogue. Prints missing from his file have been obtained from museums and private collections throughout the United States.

The catalogue that follows is in chronological order, beginning in 1917 and ending in mid-1967. Except where the prints are actually dated in plate or stone, we have relied on the artist's memory to establish the proper date for the execution of each work. When in doubt, the approximate date is given. From 1950 to the present, all dates are documented.

To the best of our knowledge, Soyer has pencil-signed all of his prints with the exception of a few trial proofs. However, he did not begin numbering each print until 1962, and the catalogue indicates those prints which have been published in numbered editions. The number of prints actually published in the earlier editions is approximate, since no records exist. These editions generally were not large, although most included a number of unrecorded trial proofs. After 1935, Soyer usually took ten artist's proofs outside of the regular edition for his own personal collection. Many of these he gave away as gifts or sold privately.

To the best of our knowledge, all plates or stones used in the execution of the prints described in this catalogue have been cancelled or effaced.

We are indebted to Mrs. Louise Weiner and Miss Estelle Yanco for contributing some of the basic research for this volume and for contacting various museums for additional information. For their always gracious help, we would like to thank Miss Elizabeth Roth of the New York Public Library, Miss Eleanor Sayre of the Boston Museum of Fine Arts, Dr. Alan Fern, Library of Congress, and Mr. Kneeland McNulty of the Philadelphia Museum of Art. We are also grateful to the following institutions and individuals who have loaned prints from their collections so that they could be photographed for inclusion in this book: Library of Congress; Museum of Fine Arts, Boston; Newark Public Library; New York Public Library; Philadelphia Museum of Art; Mr. and Mrs. Herb Davis; Mr. and Mrs. Simon Beagle; Dr. and Mrs. Lawrence Roose; Dr. and Mrs. Sam Rosen; Mr. and Mrs. Isaac Soyer. Finally, a special word of thanks to Mr. Jacob Kainen for his foreword.

Sylvan Cole, Jr.

New York, N. Y.
July 15, 1967

Contents

Raphael Soyer
fifty years of printmaking
1917–1967

The first etchings by Raphael Soyer were done in the years 1917 and 1918. Only a small press was available to him, and he personally printed the few proofs ever pulled from the plates. This press is still in the artist's studio.

PORTRAIT OF THE ARTIST'S FATHER
1917
Etching
4 x 3 in.*
Only 2 or 3 impressions
Counterproof on verso of one impression

*All measurements indicate image area, height by width.

PORTRAIT OF THE ARTIST'S MOTHER
1917
Etching
8 x 6 in.
Unique impression

SELF-PORTRAIT
1917
Etching
4 x 3 in.
Unique impression

PORTRAIT OF ISAAC SOYER
1917
Etching with black chalk
4 x 3 in.
Unique impression

Courtesy Collection Mr. and Mrs. Isaac Soyer, New York

OLD WOMAN
1917–18
Etching
$3^1/_2$ x $2^1/_2$ in.
Unique impression

Courtesy Collection Mr. and Mrs. Herb Davis, Washington, D.C.

NIGHT SCENE
c. 1917
Etching
5 x 4 in.
Only 2 or 3 impressions

During the twenties (prints seven through seventeen), Soyer began to explore lithography. His first prints in this medium were printed by Jacob Friedland and then, in the late twenties, by George Miller. It was Miller who showed him how to draw on transfer paper and then transfer the image onto the stone. Soyer still uses this method occasionally.

THE ARTIST'S FATHER
c. 1920
Lithograph. 10 x 8⅝ in.
Unique impression;
stone damaged after pulling of first proof.

SELF-PORTRAIT
c. 1920
Lithograph
First state (of two)
8³/₄ x 6¹/₄ in.
Edition: 10

SELF-PORTRAIT
c. 1920
Lithograph
Second state (of two)
8³/₄ x 6¹/₄ in.
Edition: c. 15

SAUL BERMAN
c. 1920
Lithograph
11$\frac{1}{2}$ x 10 in.
Only 3 or 4 impressions

GIRL IN STRIPED SWEATER
c. 1920
Lithograph
8$\frac{1}{4}$ x 8 in.
Edition: c. 15

THE BRONX STREET
1928
Lithograph
7 x 8³/₄ in.
Edition: 50

WILLIAMSBURG BRIDGE
1928
Lithograph
$5\frac{1}{2} \times 9$ in.
Edition: 50

EAST SIDE STREET
1928
Lithograph
7³/₄ x 10¹/₈ in.
Edition: 50

14

SUSAN
1928
Lithograph
9 x 6$\frac{1}{2}$ in.
Edition: c. 25

Susan was one of the most famous and important
artist's models in New York during the twenties.

Susan   RAPHAEL SOYER 1929

                              Raphael Soyer

EAST HOUSTON STREET
c. 1928
Lithograph
5$\frac{1}{2}$ x 9$\frac{1}{2}$ in.
Edition: 50

East Livingston St

PIKE'S SLIP
1929–30
Lithograph
5$\frac{1}{2}$ x 9 in.
Edition: c. 15

WASHINGTON SQUARE
1929–30
Lithograph
7³/₄ x 7 in.
Edition: c. 15

Washington Sq.   R Soyer

RAPHAEL SOYER

In the thirties (prints eighteen through fifty-six), Soyer continued to explore the medium of lithography. A number of major prints resulted, including The Mission and Bowery Nocturne, both completed in 1933. In 1937, the artist made several prints for the Federal Art Project of the Works Project Administration, and in 1938, he produced the lithograph Protected, the first of more than forty Soyer prints commissioned by Associated American Artists Gallery in New York.

WASHINGTON SQUARE PARK
1930
Lithograph
9 x 7 in.
Edition: c. 25

RAPHAEL SOYER

NUDE
Lithograph
1930
13 x 10$^1/_2$ in.
Only 2 or 3 impressions

Raphael Soyer,
1930

SLEEP
1931–32
Lithograph
10 x 12$\frac{1}{2}$ in.
Edition: 25

Sleep   Raphael Soyer

CONVERSATION
1931–32
Lithograph
11 x 15 in.
Edition: 25

THE JOHN REED CLUB: THE COMMITTEE
1932
Lithograph
7¼ x 10 in.
Edition: 25

Organized in the late 1920's, the John Reed Club
was composed of a group of progressive writers
and artists. The members met once a week, and
activities included discussions, lectures, and
exhibitions. Soyer joined in the early thirties
and remained until the club disbanded in the
late thirties.

Pictured left to right are: Nemo Piccoli,
Adolf Wolff, Walter Quirt, Ivar Rose,
and Anton Refregier.

THE TEAM
(also called BACKSTAGE)
c. 1932
Lithograph
14³/₄ x 11 in.
Edition: 25

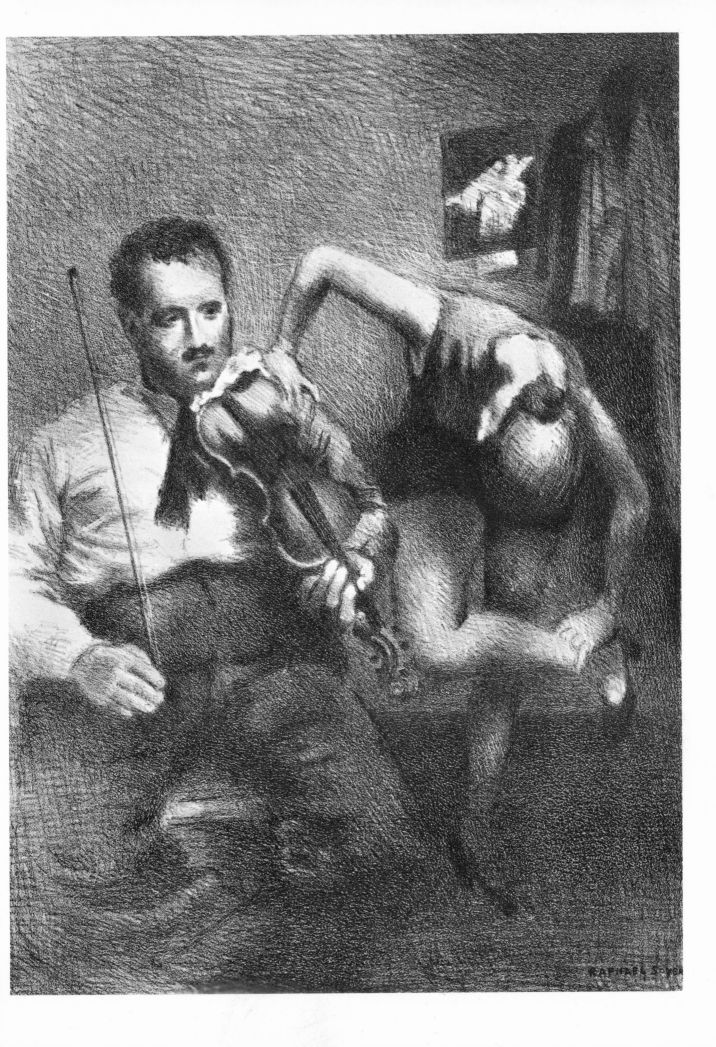

THE MODEL
c. 1932
Lithograph
16$\frac{1}{4}$ x 12 in.
Edition: 25

THE LETTER
1933
Lithograph
$14^{1}/_{4}$ x 11 in.
Edition: 25

SELF-PORTRAIT
1933
Lithograph
$13^{1}/_{4}$ x $9^{3}/_{4}$ in.
Edition: c. 25

THE MISSION
1933
Lithograph
$12^{1}/_{8} \times 17^{5}/_{8}$ in.
Edition: 25

BOWERY NOCTURNE
1933
Lithograph
$12^3/_4$ x $17^7/_8$ in.
Edition: 25

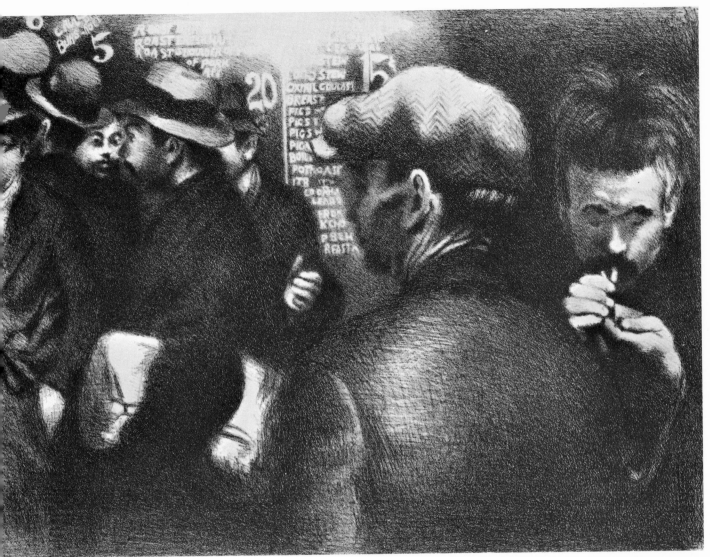

29

IN STUDIO
c. 1933
Lithograph
15 x 10¹/₄ in.
Edition: 25

SYLVIA
1933–34
Lithograph
13³/₄ x 9³/₄ in.
Edition: 25

FIGURE COMPOSITION
c. 1933
Lithograph
16 x 11$\frac{1}{2}$ in.
Edition: 25

GIRL AT TABLE
1934
Lithograph
15$\frac{1}{2}$ x 11$\frac{1}{2}$ in.
Edition: 25

TWO GIRLS
1934
Lithograph
$10^7/_8$ x $13^1/_2$ in.
Edition: 25

WATERFRONT
(aso called WATERFRONT SCENE)
1934
Lithograph
9 x 13^3/$_8$ in.
Edition: 300

This print was published by the Contemporary
Print Group, New York, as part of a portfolio
entitled *The American Scene*. Thomas Hart
Benton, John Stuart Curry, William Gropper,
Russell Limbach, and Charles Locke were the
other artists represented in this portfolio.

TOWARD THE LIGHT
1934–35
Lithograph
15$\frac{1}{4}$ x 12$\frac{1}{2}$ in.
Edition: 25

BACKSTAGE
1935
Lithograph
$15^1/_4$ x $11^1/_2$ in.
Edition: c. 30

IN STUDIO
1935
Lithograph
$13^{1}/_{2}$ x $9^{1}/_{2}$ in.
Edition: 100

OLD LABORER
c. 1935
Lithograph
9⅞ x 7 in.
Edition: 100

OLD LABORER

RAPHAEL SOYER

BEHIND THE SCREEN
c. 1935
Etching
5 x 4 in.
Only 5 impressions

PASSER-BY
c. 1935
Etching
9$\frac{1}{4}$ x 7 in.
Only 2 or 3 impressions

LAMPLIT INTERIOR
c. 1935
Etching
$7^{1}/_{4}$ x $9^{1}/_{4}$ in.
Unique impression

DANCERS RESTING
1936
Lithograph
11 x 9 in.
Edition: 250
Commissioned by American
Artists Group, New York

BACKSTAGE
c. 1937
Etching and Drypoint
8³/₈ x 6⁷/₈ in.
Edition: unknown
Executed for W.P.A.

OLD FIDDLER
1937
Etching
$9\frac{7}{8}$ x $5\frac{7}{8}$ in.
Edition: unknown
Executed for W.P.A.

OLD MAN WARMING HIS HANDS
1937
Etching
$9^{3}/_{4}$ x $5^{7}/_{8}$ in.
Edition: unknown
Executed for W.P.A.

OLD MAN
1937
Etching
9⁷/₈ x 6 in.
Edition: unknown
Executed for W.P.A.

SKETCH CLASS
1937
Etching
6 x 9$^{7}/_{8}$ in.
Edition: unknown
Executed for W.P.A.

FURNISHED ROOM
1937
Etching
7 x 8³/₄ in.
Edition: unknown
Executed for W.P.A.

A TRANSIENT
1937
Lithograph
$11^{3}/_{8} \times 9^{3}/_{8}$ in.
Edition: unknown
Executed for W.P.A.

MEN EATING
1937
Lithograph
$8^3/_4$ x $11^3/_4$ in.
Edition: unknown
Executed for W.P.A.

PUGNACITY
1937
Lithograph
$13^{1}/_{4}$ x $9^{1}/_{8}$ in.
Edition: unknown
Executed for W.P.A.

CAFETERIA
1937
Drypoint
$6^7/_8$ x $9^7/_8$ in.
Edition: unknown
Executed for W.P.A.

WORKING GIRLS GOING HOME
1937
Lithograph
11¼ x 9⅜ in.
Executed for W.P.A.

54

BEDTIME
1937
Lithograph
18 x 10¹/₄ in.
First edition: 75; second edition: 150
Commissioned by Rabin and Kreuger
Gallery, Newark, New Jersey

PROTECTED
1938
Lithograph
$13^3/_8 \times 6^1/_4$ in.
Edition: 250
Commissioned by Associated
American Artists, New York

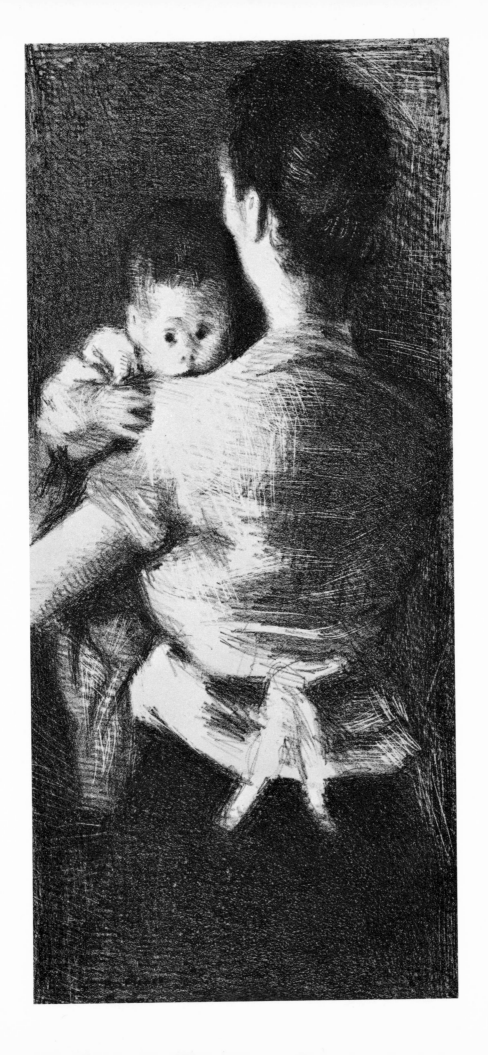

SPRINGTIME
1938
Lithograph
14 x 17$\frac{1}{4}$ in.
Edition: 25

YOUNG MODEL
1940
Lithograph
12 x 9³/₄ in.
Edition: 250
Commissioned by Associated
American Artists, New York

GIRL AT DOORWAY
1941
Etching
$9^{3}/_{4}$ x 7 in.
Edition: 250
Commissioned by Associated
American Artists, New York

WAITING
1942
Drypoint
$7^1/_8$ x $9^1/_8$ in.
Edition: 250
Commissioned by Associated
American Artists, New York

THE LAUNDRESS
1941–42
Lithograph
14$\frac{1}{2}$ x 10$\frac{3}{4}$ in.
Edition: *c.* 25

FAREWELL
(also called GOOD-BYE)
1943
Lithograph
16 x 12³/₈ in.
Edition: c. 100

62

AT THE MIRROR
1943
Lithograph
12³/₄ x 8³/₄ in.
Edition: 250
Commissioned by Associated
American Artists, New York

MY STUDIO
1944
Lithograph
12$\frac{1}{4}$ x 9$\frac{1}{2}$ in.
Edition: 250
Commissioned by Associated
American Artists, New York

THE MODEL
1944
Lithograph
11³/₄ x 7³/₄ in.
Edition: 250
Commissioned by Associated
American Artists, New York

CASTING OFFICE
1945
Lithograph
9³/₄ x 12³/₄ in.
Edition: 250
Commissioned by Associated
American Artists, New York

SLEEPING GIRL
1945
Etching
4 x 4$^7/_8$ in.
Edition: very small — number unknown

A COUPLE
c. 1946
Lithograph
13 x 9³/₄ in.
Edition c. 15

BEHIND SCREEN
(also called MODEL RESTING)
1949
Lithograph
16 x 12¼ in.
Edition: 150 (75 in black
and white, 75 in color)
Commissioned by Rabin and Kreuger
Gallery, Newark, New Jersey

This lithograph was Soyer's first print in color.
He used four stones — black, green, pale orange,
and brown — and retouched a number of
proofs by hand.

RAILROAD WAITING ROOM
1954
Lithograph
12 x 9$^1/_2$ in.
Edition: 250
Commissioned by Associated
American Artists, New York

THE WINDOW
1954
Lithograph
11 x 9½ in.
Edition: 250
Commissioned by Associated
American Artists, New York

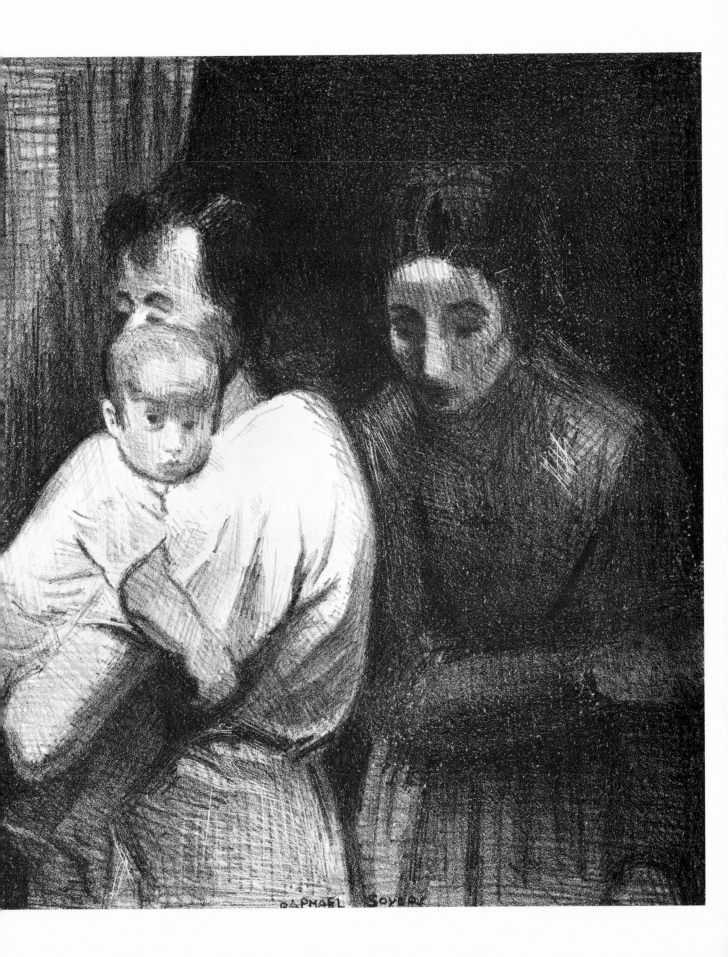

RAPHAEL SOYER

WAITRESSES
1954
Lithograph
11$\frac{1}{2}$ x 9$\frac{1}{2}$ in.
Edition: 250 (including a few
hand-colored by the artist)
Commissioned by Associated
American Artists, New York

BOY AND GIRL
1954
Lithograph
12 x 7$\frac{1}{2}$ in.
Edition: 250
Commissioned by Associated American Artists, New York

SELF-PORTRAIT
1954
Lithograph
10 x 7 in.
Edition: 250 (including a few
hand-colored by the artist)
Commissioned by Associated
American Artists, New York

RAPHAEL SOYER

DANCERS
1954
Lithograph
12 x 8 in.
Edition: 250 (including a few
hand-colored by the artist)
Commissioned by Associated
American Artists, New York

THE SEAMSTRESS
1954
Lithograph
9 x 11¾ in.
Edition: 250 (including a few
hand-colored by the artist)
Commissioned by Associated
American Artists, New York

NUDE IN INTERIOR
1954
Lithograph
12¼ x 9¼ in.
Edition: 250
Commissioned by Associated
American Artists, New York

THE DANCER
C. 1955
Lithograph
13 x 8³/₄ in.
Edition: 150 (75 in black
and white, 75 in sepia)
Commissioned by Rabin and Kreuger
Gallery, Newark, New Jersey

THE ADOLESCENT
1956
Lithograph
15^3/$_4$ x 10^3/$_4$ in.
Edition: 150 (75 in black
and white, 75 in sepia;
a few of the 150 hand-colored by the artist)
Commissioned by Rabin and Kreuger
Gallery, Newark, New Jersey

SELF-PORTRAIT
1956
Lithograph
12 x 9 in.
Edition: 150 (75 in black
and white, 75 in sepia)
Commissioned by Rabin and Kreuger
Gallery, Newark, New Jersey

RAPHAEL SOYER

GREEK GIRL #1
1959
Etching
5 x 4 in.
Edition: 200

SELF-PORTRAIT (WITH MODEL)
1959–60
Lithograph
14 x 11½ in.
Edition: 75 (including a few
hand-colored by the artist)
Commissioned by
ACA Gallery, New York

HEAD OF A GIRL
1960
Lithograph
14 x 11^1/$_8$ in
Edition: 250
Commissioned by Associated
American Artists, New York

YOUNG GIR
196
Lithograp
14$\frac{1}{4}$ x 10 in
Edition: 250
Commissioned by Associated
American Artists, New York

GIRL WITH PARTED LIPS
1962
Lithograph
13$\frac{1}{2}$ x 10 in.
Edition: 35

RAPHAEL
SOYER

THE SCREEN
1962
Lithograph
$18^{1}/_{2}$ x 14 in.
Edition: 100 numbered impressions
Commissioned by Associated
American Artists, New York

REFLECTION
1962
Lithograph
15 x 10$\frac{1}{2}$ in.
Edition: 250
Commissioned by Associated
American Artists, New York

This is a portrait of the artist's daughter, Mary.

STUDY FOR PEDESTRIANS
1962
Etching
$5^7/_8$ x $6^3/_4$ in.
Edition: c. 8

PEDESTRIANS (first plate)
1962
Etching
$9^3/_4 \times 7^3/_4$ in.
Edition: 15

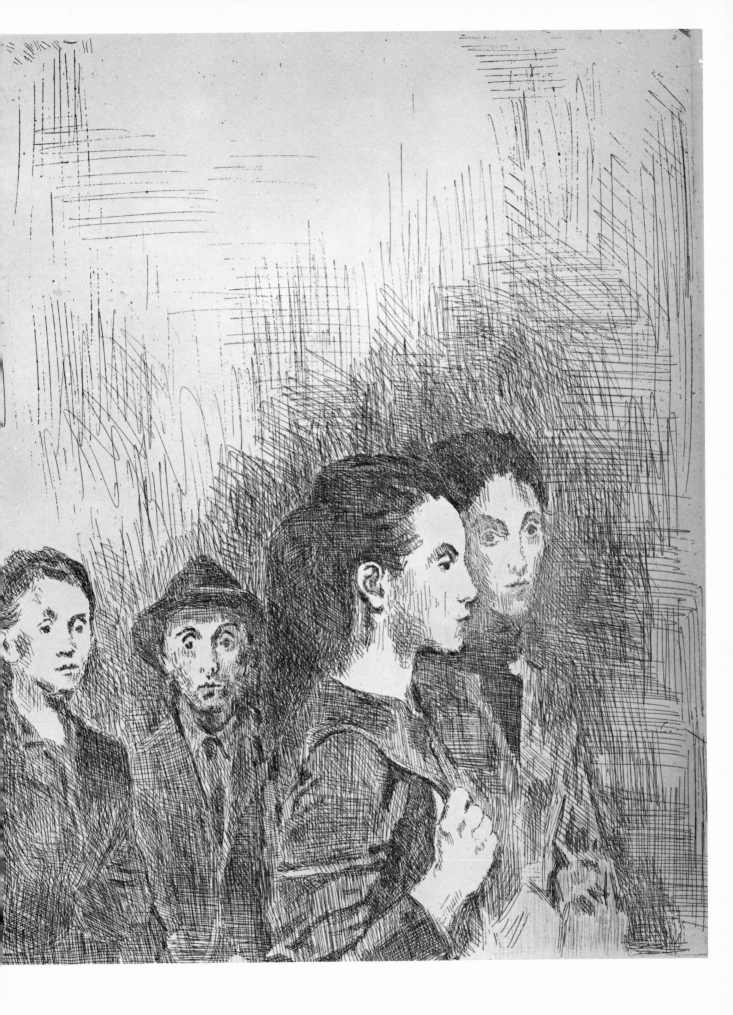

The following etchings (prints eighty-nine through one hundred and four) were done for the portfolio, Sixteen Etchings by Raphael Soyer, *published in 1965 by Associated American Artists, New York, with a foreword by Carl Zigrosser. The edition was limited to eighty-five sets. The first twenty-five, forming the deluxe suite, were printed on Japon paper and numbered 1/25 through 25/25. The next sixty were printed on Rives BFK paper and numbered 26/85 through 85/85. For each print, numbers fifty-one through eighty-five were offered separately outside of the portfolio.*

SELF-PORTRAIT
1963
Etching
4 x 2 in.
Edition: 85 numbered impressions
From portfolio, *Sixteen Etchings by Raphael Soyer,* published in 1965 by Associated American Artists, New York
Note: This print was cut from "Pedestrians (first plate)," catalogue number 88, above.

PEDESTRIANS (second plate)
1963
Etching
9³/₄ x 7³/₄ in.
Edition: 85 numbered impressions
From portfolio, *Sixteen Etchings by
Raphael Soyer,* published in 1965 by
Associated American Artists, New York

NUDE STUDIES
1963
Etching
$7^3/_4$ x $9^3/_4$ in.
Edition: 85 numbered impressions
From portfolio, *Sixteen Etchings by
Raphael Soyer*, published in 1965 by
Associated American Artists, New York

LIPSTICK
1963
Etching
9³/₄ x 7³/₄ in.
Edition: 85 numbered impressions
From portfolio, *Sixteen Etchings by
Raphael Soyer,* published in 1965 by
Associated American Artists, New York

MOTHER AND CHILD
1963
Etching
First state (of two)
9³/₄ x 7³/₄ in.
Edition: 15

MOTHER AND CHILD
1963
Etching and Aquatint
Second state (of two)
9⁷/₈ x 7³/₄ in.
Edition: 85 numbered impressions
From portfolio, *Sixteen Etchings by
Raphael Soyer,* published in 1965 by
Associated American Artists, New York

SEATED WOMAN
1963
Etching
9³/₄ x 7³/₄ in.
Edition: 85 numbered impressions
From portfolio, *Sixteen Etchings by
Raphael Soyer,* published in 1965 by
Associated American Artists, New York

PEDESTRIAN
1963
Etching
9³/₄ x 7³/₄ in.
Edition: 85 numbered impressions
From portfolio, *Sixteen Etchings by
Raphael Soyer*, published in 1965 by
Associated American Artists, New York

YOUNG WOMAN
1963
Etching and Aquatint
$9^3/_4$ x $7^3/_4$ in.
Edition: 85 numbered impressions
From portfolio, *Sixteen Etchings by Raphael Soyer,* published in 1965 by Associated American Artists, New York

WOMAN WITH A CROSS
1963
Etching and Aquatint
9³/₄ x 7³/₄ in.
Edition: 85 numbered impressions
From portfolio, *Sixteen Etchings by Raphael Soyer,* published in 1965 by
Associated American Artists, New York

GIRL WITH PARTED LIPS
1963
Etching
9³/₄ x 7³/₄ in.
Edition: 85 numbered impressions
From portfolio, *Sixteen Etchings by
Raphael Soyer,* published in 1965 by
Associated American Artists, New York

WOMAN AT TABLE
1963
Etching
$9^3/_4$ x $7^3/_4$ in.
Edition: 85 numbered impressions
From portfolio, *Sixteen Etchings by
Raphael Soyer,* published in 1965 by
Associated American Artists, New York

COUPLE IN INTERIOR
1963
Etching
$9^3/_4$ x $7^3/_4$ in.
Edition: 85 numbered impressions
From portfolio, *Sixteen Etchings by
Raphael Soyer,* published in 1965 by
Associated American Artists, New York

PENSIVE GIRL
1963
Etching
First state (of two)
9³/₄ x 7³/₄ in.
Edition: 15

PENSIVE GIRL
1963
Etching and aquatint
Second State (of two)
9³/₄ x 7³/₄ in.
Edition: 85 numbered impressions
From portfolio, *Sixteen Etchings by
Raphael Soyer,* published in 1965 by
Associated American Artists, New York

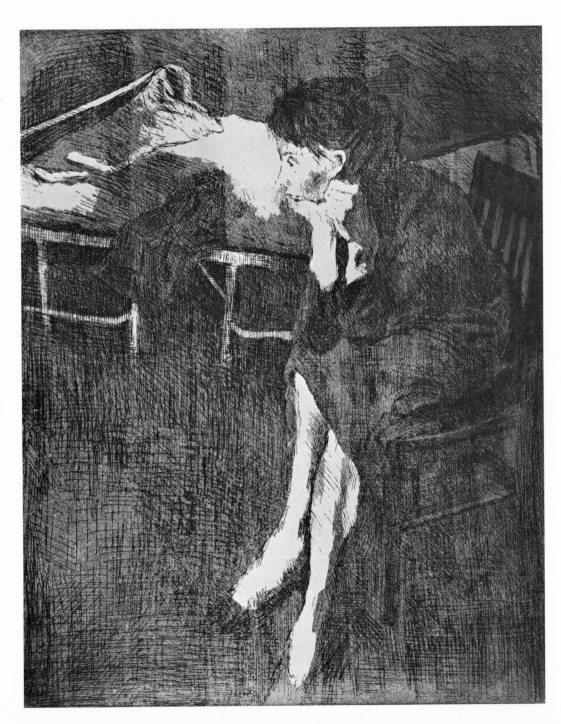

INTERIOR WITH FIGURE
1963
Etching
10 x 8 in.
Edition: 85 numbered impressions
From portfolio, *Sixteen Etchings by
Raphael Soyer,* published in 1965 by
Associated American Artists, New York

WOMAN SHADING HER EYES
1963
Etching
$9^{3}/_{4}$ x $7^{3}/_{4}$ in.
Edition: 85 numbered impressions
From portfolio, *Sixteen Etchings by
Raphael Soyer,* published in 1965 by
Associated American Artists, New York

THE ARTIST'S PARENTS
1963
Etching
First state (of two)
7³/₄ x 9³/₄ in.
Edition: 5

THE ARTIST'S PARENTS
1963
Etching and aquatint
Second state (of two)
7¹/₄ x 7³/₄ in.
Edition: 85 numbered impressions
From portfolio, *Sixteen Etchings by
Raphael Soyer*, published in 1965 by
Associated American Artists, New York

ARTIST AND MODEL
1963
Serigraph
30 x 19^1/$_2$ in.
Edition: 40 numbered impressions

This is Soyer's only serigraph to date. It was
printed by Steve Poleskie and was signed by him
("Poleskie/imp.") as well as by Soyer.

Raphael Soyer

MOTHER AND CHILD
1964
Color Lithograph
$17^{3}/_{4}$ x 14 in.
Edition: 100 numbered impressions. (A few
unnumbered black and white proofs also were pulled.)
Commissioned by the Vincent Price Collection,
Sears Roebuck and Company, Chicago

SELF-PORTRAIT (WITH WIFE)
1964
Etching
$7^{7}/_{8} \times 9^{3}/_{4}$ in.
Edition: C. 50

PORTRAIT OF CHRIS
(also called PROFILE)
1965
Lithograph
$17^{1}/_{4}$ x $12^{3}/_{4}$ in.
Edition: 100 numbered impressions
Commissioned by Yamet Fine Arts, New York

RAPHAEL SOYER

SING A SONG OF FRIENDSHIP
1965–66
Lithograph
14 x 12³/₄ in.
Edition: 300 numbered impressions.
Commissioned by the Benrus Company, New York

GREEK GIRL #2
1966
Etching
$10^3/_4 \times 8^1/_2$ in.
Edition: 100 numbered impressions
Commissioned by Associated
American Artists, New York

GREEK GIRL #3
1966
Etching
7 x 5¼ in.
Edition: 100 numbered impressions
Commissioned by Associated American
Artists, New York, for the deluxe
edition of this volume

YOUNG DANCERS
1966
Lithograph
17 x 13 in.
Edition: 100 numbered impressions
Commissioned by Associated
American Artists, New York

NUDES
1966
Lithograph
20 x 23 in.
Edition: 100 numbered impressions
(50 in black and white, 50 in sepia)
Commissioned by the Grippi Gallery, New York

MOTHER AND CHILD
1966
Lithograph
16 x 22 in.
Edition: 50 numbered impressions
(25 in black and white, 25 in sepia)

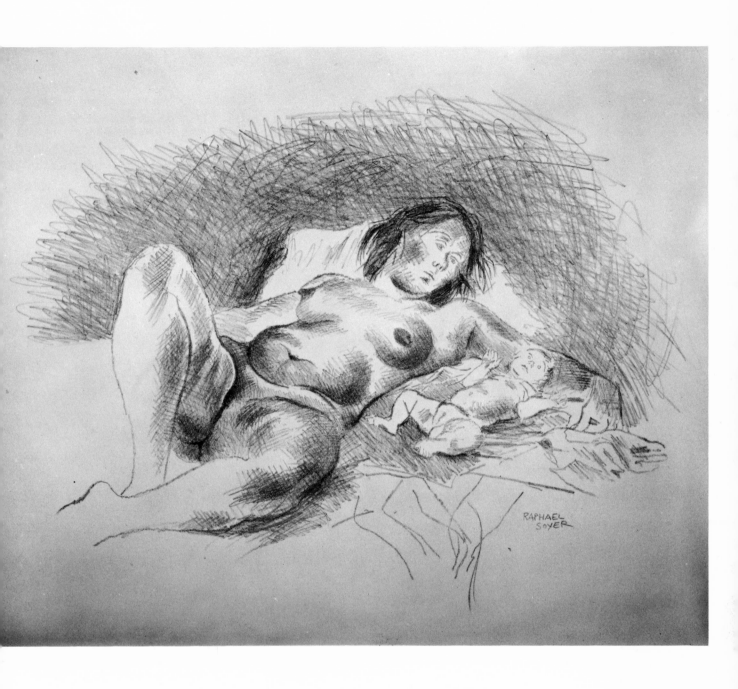

STUDIES WITH SELF-PORTRAIT
1966
Lithograph
First state (of two)
21 x 24 in.
Edition: 100 numbered impressions
Commissioned by Associated
American Artists, New York

STUDIES WITH SELF-PORTRAIT
1967
Lithograph
Second state (of two)
22 x 28½ in.
Edition: 50 numbered impressions
Commissioned by Associated
American Artists, New York

116

SELF-PORTRAIT
1967
Lithograph
First state (of two)
10 x 8¹/₄ in.
Edition: 25 numbered impressions
Commissioned by Associated
American Artists, New York

SELF-PORTRAIT
1967
Lithograph
Second state (of two)
10 x 8¹/₄ in.
Edition: 50 numbered impressions
Commissioned by Associated
American Artists, New York

SELF-PORTRAIT (WITH WIFE)
1967
Lithograph
First state (of two)
11 x 15 in.
Edition: 25 numbered impressions
Commissioned by Associated
American Artists, New York

SELF-PORTRAIT (WITH WIFE)
1967
Lithograph
Second state (of two)
11 x 15 in.
Edition: 25 numbered impressions
Commissioned by Associated
American Artists, New York

JAPANESE GIRL
1967
Lithograph
9 x 15¹/₄ in.
Edition: 40 numbered impressions
Commissioned by Associated
American Artists, New York

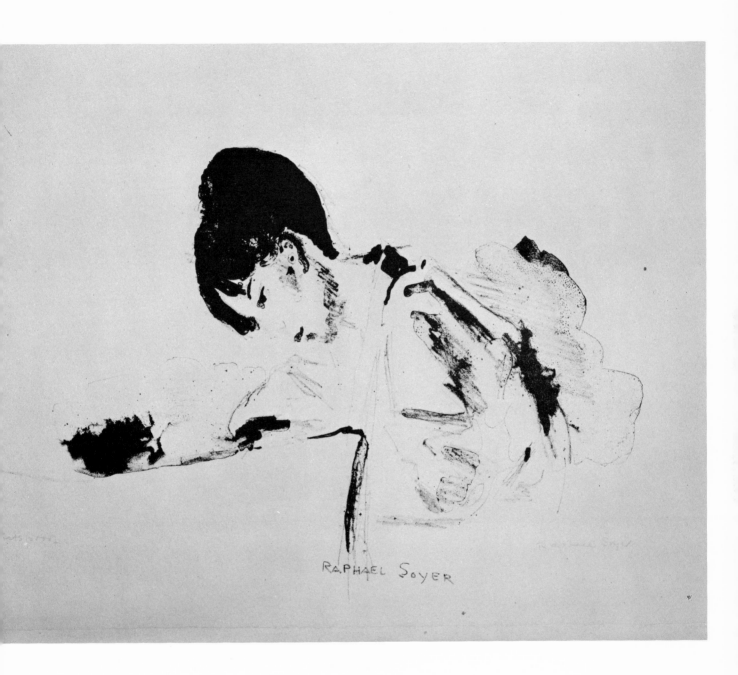

RAPHAEL SOYER

MAN AND WIFE
1967
Lithograph
14 x 21$^1/_2$ in.
Edition: 25 numbered impressions
Commissioned by Associated
American Artists, New York

MOTHER AND CHILD
1967
Color Lithograph
14 x 10^{1}/$_{2}$
Edition: 25 numbered impressions
Created for the Spanish Refugee
Committee, New York

WOMAN SHADING HER EYES
1967
Lithograph
$15^{1}/_{4}$ x $11^{1}/_{8}$ in.
Edition: 50 numbered impressions
Created for Brandeis University
National Woman's Committee,
Gotham Chapter (New York)

PORTRAIT OF JOAN
1967
Lithograph
$14^3/_4$ x $10^1/_2$ in.
Edition: 100 numbered impressions
Commissioned by Associated
American Artists, New York

GIRL IN BLACK STOCKINGS
1967
Lithograph
18 x 16$^{1}/_{2}$ in.
Edition: 100 numbered impressions
Commissioned by Associated
American Artists, New York

FIGURE STUDIES
1967
Lithograph
18 x 22 in.
Edition: 50 numbered impressions
(25 in black and white, 25 in sepia)
Commissioned by Associated
American Artists, New York

LOVERS, ETC.
1967
Lithograph
18 x 22 in.
Edition: 50 numbered impressions
(25 in black and white, 25 in sepia)

BOY WITH RECORDER
1967
Lithograph
$8^{1}/_{2}$ x 6 in.
Frontispiece to this volume

Index of prints

RAPHAEL SOYER

BORN
December 25, 1899, in Tombov, Russia

STUDIED
Cooper Union, New York
National Academy of Design, New York
Art Students' League, New York

ONE-MAN EXHIBITIONS
Daniel Gallery, New York, 1929
L'Elan Gallery, New York, 1932
Curt Valentin Gallery, New York, 1933, 34, 35, 37, 38
Frank K. M. Rehn Gallery, New York, 1939
Associated American Artists Gallery, New York, 1940, 41, 48, 53, 55, 64, 67
Weyhe Gallery, New York, 1944
Philadelphia Art Alliance, 1949
ACA Gallery, New York, 1960
Alfredo Valente Gallery, New York, 1961
Bernard Crystal Gallery, New York, 1962
Forum Gallery, New York, 1964, 66, 67
Retrospective Exhibition, Whitney Museum of American Art, New York, 1967

GROUP EXHIBITIONS
Salons of America, New York, 1926
Pennsylvania Academy of the Fine Arts, Philadelphia, 1934, 43, 46
Corcoran Gallery, Washington, D.C., 1937, 51
Virginia Museum of Fine Arts, Richmond, Virginia, 1938
Art Institute of Chicago, 1940
Brooklyn Museum, 1941
Carnegie Institute, Pittsburgh, 1944
Phillips Gallery, Washington, D.C., 1944
Dallas Museum of Fine Arts, 1945
California Palace of the Legion of Honor, San Francisco, 1945
Museum of Modern Art, New York, 1946
National Academy of Design, New York, 1951, 52
Whitney Museum of American Art, New York, Annuals, from 1932

AWARDS
Carnegie Institute, Pittsburgh, Honorable Mention Award (three times)
Art Institute of Chicago, Norman Wait Harris Gold Medal, 1932
Pennsylvania Academy of the Fine Arts, Philadelphia, Carol H. Beck Gold Medal, 1934
Art Institute of Chicago, Norman Wait Harris Bronze Medal, 1940
Pennsylvania Academy of the Fine Arts, Philadelphia,
Joseph H. Temple Gold Medal, 1943
Pennsylvania Academy of the Fine Arts, Philadelphia, Walter Lippincott Prize, 1946
Corcoran Gallery, Washington, D.C.,

William A. Clark Prize and Corcoran Gold Medal, 1951
National Institute of Arts and Letters Grant, 1945
First Prize, ART USA, 1959

COLLECTIONS (partial listing)
Addison Gallery of American Art, Andover, Massachusetts
Albright–Knox Art Gallery, Buffalo, New York
Boston Museum of Fine Arts
Brooklyn Museum
Butler Institute of American Art, Youngstown, Ohio
Chrysler Museum, Provincetown, Massachusetts
Columbus Gallery of Fine Arts, Columbus, Ohio
Corcoran Gallery, Washington, D.C.
Detroit Museum of Fine Art
Metropolitan Museum of Art, New York
Montclair Museum, Montclair, New Jersey
Museum of Modern Art, New York
Newark Museum, Newark, New Jersey
New York Public Library
Pennsylvania Academy of the Fine Arts, Philadelphia
Philadelphia Museum of Art
Phillips Memorial Gallery, Washington, D.C.
Wadsworth Atheneum, Hartford, Connecticut
Whitney Museum of American Art, New York

MEMBER
National Academy of Design
National Institute of Arts and Letters

TEACHING ACTIVITIES
Art Students' League, New York
American Artists School, New York
New School for Social Research, New York
National Academy of Design, New York

PUBLICATIONS

BY THE ARTIST:
A Painter's Pilgrimage: An Account of a Journey.
  New York, Crown Publishers, 1962.
Homage to Thomas Eakins, Etc., edited by Rebecca L. Soyer.
  South Brunswick, New Jersey, Thomas Yoseleff, 1966.

ABOUT THE ARTIST:
Raphael Soyer. New York, American Artists Group, 1946.
Raphael Soyer, Paintings and Drawings. Text by Walter K. Gutman,
        preface by Jerome Klein. New York, Shorewood Publishing Co., 1960.

Printers

Andersen–Lamb Company	58,59
Jacob Friedland	7,8,9,10,17,18,19,22
Irwin Hollander	115,116,117,118,119,120,123
Burr Miller	82,83,84,85,86,106,108,109, 112,113,114,121,122,124,125, 126
George Miller	11,12,13,14,20,21,23,24,25,26, 27,29,30,31,32,33,34,35,36,37, 38,42,54,55,56,57,60,61,62,63, 64,65,66,68,69,70,71,72,73,74, 75,76,77,78,79
Steve Poleskie	105
Emiliano Sorini	80,81,88,89,90,91,92,93,94,95, 96,97,98,99,100,101,102,103, 104,107,110,111.